CONSERVATION CHAMPIONS!

REDUCING WASTE

SADIE SILVA

Enslow PUBLISHING

Please visit our website, www.enslow.com.
For a free color catalog of all our high-quality books, call toll free 1-800-398-2504 or fax 1-877-980-4454.

Library of Congress Cataloging-in-Publication Data
Names: Silva, Sadie author
Title: Reducing waste / Sadie Silva.
Description: Buffalo, NY : Enslow Publishing, [2027] | Series: Conservation champions! | Includes index.
Identifiers: LCCN 2025049082 (print) | LCCN 2025049083 (ebook) | ISBN 9781978547773 library binding | ISBN 9781978547766 paperback | ISBN 9781978547780 ebook
Subjects: LCSH: Waste minimization | Conservation of natural resources | Refuse and refuse disposal | Recycling (Waste, etc.)
Classification: LCC TD793.9 .S55 2027 (print) | LCC TD793.9 (ebook) | DDC 363.72/8–dc23/eng/20260309
LC record available at https://lccn.loc.gov/2025049082
LC ebook record available at https://lccn.loc.gov/2025049083

Published in 2027 by
Enslow Publishing
2544 Clinton Street
Buffalo, NY 14224

Designer: Tanya Dellaccio Keeney
Editor: Therese Shea

Photo credits: cover (bottles) iamshutter/Shutterstock.com; cover (kid) myboys.me/Shutterstock.com; p. 5 Tony Stock/Shutterstock.com; p. 7 Phovoir/Shutterstock.com; p. 9 (landfill) MOHAMED ABDULRAHEEM/Shutterstock.com; p. 9 (batteries) alina_stor/Shutterstock.com; p. 11 (paper) Anton Watman/Shutterstock.com; p. 11 (forest) Alex Konon/Shutterastock.com; p. 13 (plastic straws and spoons) SmLyubov/Shutterstock.com; p. 13 (diapers) SoNelly/Shutterstock.com; p. 15 Thijs de Graaf/Shutterstock.com; p. 17 Volurol/Shutterstock.com; p. 19 PRASANNAPIX/Shutterstock.com; p. 21 Pumbastyle/Shutterstock.com.

Printed in the United States of America

CPSIA compliance information: Batch #CSENS27: For further information contact Enslow Publishing, at 1-800-398-2504.

CONTENTS

BOLDFACE WORDS APPEAR IN THE GLOSSARY.

THAT'S WASTEFUL!

Have you ever used a plastic water bottle? What did you do with it when you were done? Many people throw it into the trash. That's wasteful! You can help save Earth by reducing waste. You can be a conservation champion!

YOU CAN USE A METAL BOTTLE OVER AND OVER. THAT HELPS REDUCE WASTE!

WHAT IS CONSERVATION?

Conservation means helping Earth. It means taking care of the **resources** Earth gives us. We should use them wisely and make sure they don't run out. We need to cut down on waste and **pollution**.

SOME RESOURCES ARE NONRENEWABLE—THAT MEANS WHEN WE RUN OUT, THERE'S NO MORE TO BE FOUND.

WHAT IS WASTE?

Waste is anything that is thrown away. We throw away old napkins, toys, clothes, and food. When something is put in the trash, it won't be used again. It will probably go to a **landfill**. This is not good for Earth. Landfills pollute the **environment**.

TOXIC THINGS LIKE BATTERIES ARE VERY BAD FOR THE ENVIRONMENT WHEN THEY'RE THROWN IN THE TRASH.

LANDFILL

USING TOO MUCH

Waste makes us use more resources. If you throw away a plastic bottle, you may use another—and another after that! If you throw away clothes or phones after they "go out of style," this uses more materials. We have to take more from Earth.

TREES ARE CUT DOWN TO MAKE PAPER AND WOODEN PRODUCTS. THAT HARMS ANIMAL HOMES.

SAY NO TO SINGLE USE

"Single use" goods are meant to be thrown away after use. Examples include plastic bottles, plastic bags, diapers, and food **packaging**. Some plastic forks and spoons are also **disposable**. You can say no to single use! You can use reusable bottles, **cutlery**, and bags.

AROUND 300,000 DIAPERS ARE THROWN OUT EVERY MINUTE AROUND THE WORLD. THEY LAST UP TO 500 YEARS IN LANDFILLS.

CONSERVE WATER

You can also reduce waste when using water. Humans use a lot of fresh water. Some people and animals don't have enough. To conserve water, you can take short showers. Never leave water running. Only water your plants as much as they need.

YOU CAN CATCH FRESH WATER IN A RAIN BARREL TO WATER YOUR PLANTS!

GET CREATIVE!

Use the resources you already have. Instead of throwing out an old toy and buying another, swap it with a friend. Buy clothes secondhand. Donate old clothes and toys. Use what you have before you buy something new.

THINK BEFORE YOU BUY! YOU MAY ALREADY HAVE WHAT YOU NEED AT HOME.

YOU CAN BE A CHAMPION!

Waste is bad for Earth. It causes pollution. It makes some resources **scarce**. But you can be a conservation champion! You can use what you have. You can think before you buy. You can reuse things, trade things, and get creative.

BEFORE YOU GET SOMETHING NEW, THINK: "DO I REALLY NEED THAT?"

ACTIVITY

- For one day, keep track of everything you throw in the trash. Look at your list. Choose one thing from the list that you often throw out.
- Ask yourself: Did I have to throw that out? If yes, ask: What could I use instead?
- For example, if you throw out a lot of paper towels, you could use real towels to clean up messes. If you use plastic bottles, you could get a reusable bottle.

GLOSSARY

cutlery: Tools for cutting and eating food.

disposable: Made to be thrown away after use.

environment: The natural world.

landfill: An area where waste is buried.

packaging: Something used to contain something else.

pollution: The act of water or land becoming unsafe for people or animals.

resource: A usable supply of something.

scarce: A very small amount.

FOR MORE INFORMATION

BOOKS

Bergin, Raymond. *Minimizing Waste*. Minneapolis, MN: Bearport Publishing, 2025.

Holmes, Kirsty. *Reduce, Reuse, Recycle*. Buffalo, NY: KidHaven Publishing, 2024.

WEBSITES

Reduce Waste
www.niehs.nih.gov/health/kids/topics/reduce/reduce-waste
Learn more tips about reducing waste with the National Institute of Environmental Health Sciences.

Reducing and Reusing Waste
www.epa.gov/recycle/reducing-and-reusing-basics
Check out some great ideas for reducing and reusing in your everyday life.

Publisher's note to educators and parents: Our editors have carefully reviewed these websites to ensure that they are suitable for students. Many websites change frequently, however, and we cannot guarantee that a site's future contents will continue to meet our high standards of quality and educational value. Be advised that students should be closely supervised whenever they access the internet.

INDEX